WORLD OF WOW WONDER

SEE HOW THEY WORK &
LOOK INSIDE
FARM EQUIPMENT

Have you ever wondered where our food comes from? Farmers work hard all through the year to grow and raise the food we eat. Some farmers grow corn or other crops, while other farmers raise animals. Each different type of farm has its own special equipment it needs for the tasks at hand, from plowing, to harvesting, to just having fun! Farm machines are pretty amazing!

© 2015 Flowerpot Press

Contents under license from Aladdin Books Ltd.

Flowerpot Press
142 2nd Avenue North
Franklin, TN 37064

Flowerpot Press is a Division of Kamalu LLC, Franklin, TN, U.S.A.
and Flowerpot Children's Press Inc., Oakville, ON, Canada.

ISBN: 978-1-4867-0803-1

Editor: Michael Flaherty

Design: David West Children's Book Design

Designer: Simon Morse

Illustrators: Simon Tegg & Ross Watton

American Edition Editors: Johannah Gilman Paiva
                          and Ashley Rideout

American Redesign: Stephanie Meyers

Consultants: Paul and Denise Fantozzi

Printed in China.

TABLE OF CONTENTS

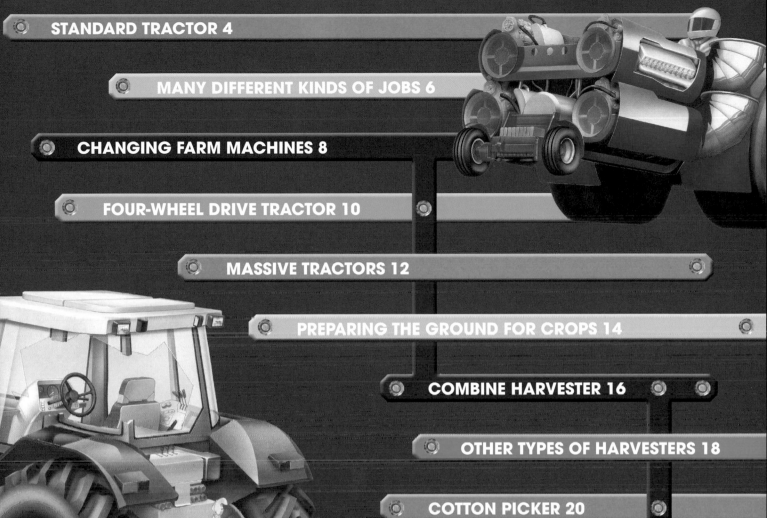

STANDARD TRACTOR

Around the farm, farmers need machines that can perform many different roles, from pulling trailers to clearing out milking sheds. The machine that fits this job is the tractor. It can lift and drag heavy objects around the farmyard, and is also tough enough to drive across rugged countryside in all weather conditions. The driver's cab is fitted with a tough roll cage to protect the driver if the tractor should tip over.

Many gears

Tractors have to be able to drive over many different surfaces, including dry farmyards and muddy fields. To handle these, tractors have many gears to help deliver the power needed from the engine to the drive shaft and the wheels. Some tractors have 18 forward gears and six reverse gears!

HANDY MACHINE

Tractors like this one (above) can be seen on farms all over the country being used to clear land, plow, plant, or harvest depending on what tool is attached.

Front wheels

The front wheels of this tractor are much smaller than its rear wheels. These small front wheels are not powered by the engine, but are just used for steering.

Chunky wheels

The big rear wheels with their chunky tread help the tractor to drive over uneven ground. They also spread the tractor's weight over a larger area. This stops it from squashing the soil, which could harm a growing crop.

Cushion comfort

Some cabs have seats that have air-filled cushions. These cushions absorb knocks and jolts, giving the farmer a more comfortable ride.

Attachment points

Farm machines, such as plows and seed drills, are connected to attachment points on the tractor. The hydraulic linkage can be raised and lowered to hold the machine at the correct height. The power takeoff (PTO) transfers power from the tractor to the machine.

MANY DIFFERENT KINDS OF JOBS

A tractor can do all sorts of useful jobs on a farm, depending on what type of tool is attached to it. This makes tractors the biggest multi-purpose vehicle on the farm! John Froelich, a blacksmith from Iowa, built the first successful gasoline-powered tractor in 1892. It was the first gas powered tractor able to move forward and backward and was used for threshing wheat. Before this, threshing machines had been heavy and hard to use, and there was even a risk of sparks from the boiler starting a fire. Froelich's machine made farming much safer and was the beginning stage of the tractor that we use today. Now there are nearly 17 million tractors in use in the world!

GOING UP

The front of this tractor (below) has been fitted with two powerful hydraulic arms to lift heavy objects. In this case, they are being used to lift and stack bales of hay (see pages 22-23). The other tractor is linked up to a trailer and is waiting to tow the hay bales away.

TOWING A TRAILER

The simplest job a tractor does is towing. Even the smallest tractors are used to pull trailers (left). These trailers can contain anything, from harvested crops to manure.

IN THE DARK

Some jobs on the farm may need to be done at any time—even in the middle of the night! Some crops like lettuce and grapes are so perishable, they have to be picked right away, so farmers pick all through the night to get them picked at just the right time. Other times, farmers have more crops than they can pick during the day and have to work through the nighttime. To work in the dark, tractors are fitted with headlights (right). At least it's cooler when the sun is down!

LEAF BLOWING

Tractors are not only used on farms. This tractor (left) is being used on a golf course. It is pushing a machine that cuts the grass evenly.

CHANGING FARM MACHINES

Farm machines have progressed from being pulled by animals, to being powered by steam, to now being powered by gas and hydraulics. Though today's machines are far more efficient than those of the past, their creation would never have been possible without the inventions that came before them.

ANIMAL POWER

Before steam engines were invented, farm machines, such as plows, were pulled by animals, including horses and cows (left). Animals are still used on farms in many parts of the world today.

ALL-PURPOSE MACHINE

Although not as powerful as today's tractors, the first gasoline-powered tractors (left) changed farming a great deal. They were faster and more powerful than animals, and allowed farmers to farm more in less time. The first tractors to use gasoline engines were introduced in the 1890s.

ENGINE POWER

In the late 1930s, engineer Harry Ferguson (right) invented the hydraulic linkage that connected farm machinery to the tractor. It lets the farmer move and use machinery from the tractor's seat. The basic design for this is still used today (see pages 4-5).

STEAM THRESHING

Some of the earliest farm engines were powered by steam. Here (left), a steam traction engine is powering a threshing machine to separate the grain from the straw.

FOUR-WHEEL DRIVE TRACTOR

Some of the most powerful farm tractors have four-wheel drive. This means that all four wheels are powered by the engine, instead of just the back two wheels, as in the standard tractor (see pages 4-5). Four-wheel drive allows the tractor to travel over the muddiest terrain.

Computer control

Inside the driver's cab is a computer that tells the farmer how the tractor is performing. Because the tractor's wheels might slip in the muddy conditions, the tractor also uses a radar system that tells the driver the tractor's exact speed.

Cleaner engines

Today's tractor engines work efficiently, saving farmers money on fuel. Efficient engines also give off lower levels of harmful exhaust gases, helping to keep the environment cleaner.

Front attachments

This tractor also has attachment points on its front. This means that a farmer can power and control more than one machine at the same time.

This four-wheel drive tractor (above) also has a special suspension system that allows it to drive on roads at speeds of up to 50 miles (80 kilometers) per hour—nearly twice as fast as other tractors!

Rear strength

The back of this tractor can lift a load of over three tons (2.7 metric tons)—about the weight of a fully grown elephant!

Special suspension

The rear wheels on most tractors are linked by a solid rear axle that has little or no suspension. This means that they cannot absorb bumps in the ground very well, so the ride is pretty bumpy! All four wheels on this tractor, however, have independent suspension. This reduces the vibration, allowing it to drive faster on all surfaces.

MASSIVE TRACTORS

The bigger a tractor, the more powerful it is, but this power comes at a price. When a tractor gets larger, it also becomes slower because it requires much more energy to move that much weight. The slower speed can be a good thing, though, because it allows the farmer to pay attention to the heavy load and make sure that the weight doesn't pull the tractor over.

TREMENDOUS TRACTORS

This tractor (below) needs to be powerful to handle a huge farm. The largest tractor engines can generate 525 horsepower—almost as much as a Formula One racing car!

◎ MONSTER MACHINES

The largest tractors in the world, such as this one from Canada (right), can weigh nearly 22 tons (20 metric tons)—that's as much as about 340 adults!

DOUBLE WHEELS ◎

To stop the heaviest tractors from squashing and damaging the soil, many of them are fitted with double wheels (left). These spread the tractor's weight over a greater area, making the tractor more gentle on the ground. There are four sets of twin wheels to carry the heavy load as well as two wheels to steer with at the front.

PREPARING THE GROUND FOR CROPS

There are many things a farmer needs to do to prepare a field for crops, including plowing, rolling, cultivating, and planting the seeds. The machines that do these things have changed a great deal over time. The first steel plow was invented In 1837 by an American blacksmith named John Deere. Earlier iron plows got caked in mud, but mud slipped off the new steel plow blades, creating a cleaner furrow in which seeds could be planted. Another successful first was the mechanical seed drill, invented in 1701 by an English farmer named Jethro Tull. It was pulled behind a horse and dropped the seeds into neat rows to improve the efficiency of the planting process. With so many steps necessary for farmers to grow crops, it's helpful to have modern machines to make these jobs easier!

PLOWING

Before the farmer can plant a crop, the ground must be prepared. The metal blades of a plow, or cultivator, are pulled through the ground by a tractor (left). These blades break up the soil, making it easier for the farmer to prepare the earth.

ROLLING

To prepare the soil even further, a farmer uses a roller (right). Rollers are made up of a number of wide metal rings that are pulled behind a tractor. As the roller moves over the ground, these rings break up any clumps of earth, push any stones into the ground, and squash the soil down to create a good surface for planting. An even, smooth ground helps every bit of the field be ready for growing!

SEED DRILL

The farmer plants the crop using a seed drill (above). The seeds are held in a large container. As the seed drill is pulled along, the seeds are fed through pipes and dropped into small channels that are cut in the earth by small prongs in front of the pipes. The seeds and the channels are then covered with soil by more small prongs at the rear of the seed drill.

CULTIVATOR

As well as plowing a field, a farmer can use a cultivator (left) to prepare the ground. Cultivators have a number of prongs or blades that are moved through the soil to break it up even more. By breaking up the soil before the crops are planted, cultivators allow more air and water to seep into the earth. This helps the crops to grow.

COMBINE HARVESTER

When it comes to harvesting a crop, farmers today have machines that can do the same jobs that used to take hundreds of farm laborers. Combine harvesters can cut the crop and sort the grain out from the straw and waste matter, or chaff. Some of the largest combine harvesters can cut a strip that is 23 feet (7 meters) wide—as much as four adults lying head-to-toe.

Cutting

The large reel at the front feeds the crop onto a moving, serrated blade. After the crop is cut, an auger feeds it onto the crop elevator, which carries it into the harvester for threshing.

Satellite navigation

Some of the most modern harvesters are fitted with a link to satellites orbiting the Earth. These satellites tell the farmer exactly where the harvester is positioned. From this, the farmer can figure out how much land he or she has harvested.

Emptying the load

When the grain tank is full, it is emptied into trucks through this long unloader spout.

Threshing

Inside the harvester is the threshing drum. This has tough metal bars that spin around to beat the crop and separate the grain from the unusable portion of the plant, the chaff.

Separating the crop

After the threshing drum, the crop passes onto the "straw walkers." As the crop moves along these, the grain falls through sieves and is moved to the grain tank at the top of the harvester. The straw passes up and out of the back of the harvester and the lightweight chaff is blown off the grain using a fan.

⚙ LEAVING THE STRAW

Some combine harvesters, like this one (right), have a mechanism that spreads the leftover straw over a large area to prevent it from piling up. Then, the straw is picked up by another machine to be rolled into a bale.

OTHER TYPES OF HARVESTERS

There are many other types of harvesters, perfect for the specific crop they are made to harvest. The first successful harvesting machine was invented in 1834 by an American farmer named Cyrus Hall McCormick. The McCormick Reaper was pulled by a horse team and used to separate grain from the rest of the plant that was left standing behind the machine after it went by. Two American brothers, John and Hiram Pitts, invented a threshing machine in 1837 that was able to separate 300 to 500 bushels a day.

CUTTING CORN

Some combine harvesters can be fitted with different types of cutting tools to cut different crops, such as sunflowers. Here (left), one is harvesting a crop of corn.

BURIED TREASURE

Many crops grow underground, including sugar beets and potatoes. They need special harvesters to collect them. This machine (below) cuts off the green parts of the plants that grow above ground, and then digs the roots out from the earth.

PICKING GRAPES

Grapes grow on vines—climbing plants that farmers grow in rows. A grape harvester (right) is a special machine that drives along between the vines, gently rubbing the grapes off the vine, so that they can be used to make wine.

IN A PADDY

This small harvester (left) is used to harvest rice. It is made to drive through the flooded rice fields, called "paddies." The harvester has to be small and light to keep it from sinking into the paddies.

COTTON PICKER

The invention of the cotton gin by American Eli Whitney in 1793 allowed farmers to grow cotton on a large scale for the first time. Cotton plants produce balls of fluffy cotton, called "cotton bolls." The bolls grow on a sharp spike that makes them painful to pick by hand. Today, huge machines called "cotton pickers" are used to harvest the cotton bolls, making the process faster and much less painful. These enormous pickers strip the cotton bolls off the plant and collect them in a huge basket at the back.

Blowing cotton
Powerful fans at the front blow the picked cotton up through chutes and into the basket.

Expanding basket
The roof of the basket, in which the cotton bolls are collected, rises in stages so the picker can hold more cotton.

Engine power
This cotton picker is fitted with a powerful engine. This engine powers the pickers at the front of the machine and helps to squash the cotton bolls after they've been picked.

Automatic steering

This cotton picker is fitted with a special guidance system that steers the machine automatically. This lets the operator concentrate on picking the cotton rather than on keeping the picker on course.

TAKING OUT THE SEEDS

The cotton from this picker (above) will be used to make thread that can be woven to make clothes, carpets, and blankets.

Spinning spikes

The pickers at the front of the machine are made up of spiked drums. As these drums spin, the spikes tear the buds of cotton away from the plant.

Up and down

There are special sensors at the front of the cotton picker that detect changes in ground height. The pickers can then move up and down automatically so they stay at the correct height. This ensures that they pick as much of the crop as possible.

HAY BALER

After a crop has been harvested, the farmer is left with a field covered with the stems of the cut plants. This is called either "hay," which can be used to feed animals, or "straw," which is used as bedding for animals. Once the hay or straw has dried properly, the farmer uses a hay baler to collect it into parcels called "bales." Bales can be either round or square.

Tractor power
The hay baler is pulled by a tractor. The tractor also supplies the power that makes the hay baler work.

Collecting straw
At the front of the hay baler is a pronged drum. As this drum rotates, it picks up the hay or straw from the ground and feeds it into the baler.

Rollers

As hay is fed into the bale chamber, steel rollers around the wall of the chamber roll the hay into a large, round bale.

The hay baler (above) drops a bale behind once it has gathered and rolled enough straw. Once the baler is done, the field will have many bales left behind to be gathered.

Round bale

Round bales are better at shedding water than square bales. A large, round hay bale can weigh as much as 1,100 pounds (500 kilograms)—that's as much as about seven adults!

Back passage

Once the bale is big enough, the machine wraps it in twine. Then, the rear of the baler is opened and the bale rolls down a ramp and out of the machine.

MAKING FOOD FOR ANIMALS

Farm animals need their food to be gathered just like people. Farmers plant and select specific plants to make animal food, called "fodder," out of so that the animals will grow big and strong. This fodder comes from grass or from crops that are not yet ripe. Farmers will make sure to gather and store enough fodder to last through the winter months when crops don't grow.

GREEN CROPS

Farmers make fodder, which is used to feed animals, from green or unripe crops. These green crops can include grass or unripe corn. Here (right), unripe corn is being cut and pulped along with its stalks.

CUTTING GRASS

Here (below), a tractor is powering a cutter to chop down grass. As the cutter moves forward, huge blades spin around, cutting the grass. This cut grass is then funneled into rows, called "swaths," that make it easier to collect. However, before the grass is collected to make fodder, the farmer leaves the swaths out for a day or two so the grass wilts a little. These swaths are then collected using a forage harvester (see top right).

COLLECTING THE GRASS

As the forage harvester moves forward, the spiked drum at the front picks up the swath and feeds it into the machine (above). Here, the grass is chopped up finely before it is fed into a waiting trailer and carried off for storage.

SILAGE CLAMP

The green crops have to be stored and fermented before they turn into silage ready for animals to eat. They can be stored in large towers called "silos," open yards called "silage clamps" (right), or pits. They can also be collected into bales and wrapped in plastic.

TRACTOR PULLING

Tractor pulling developed from competitions between farmers to see who had the strongest tractor. Today, it has become the most powerful motor sport in the world. Tractor drivers compete to see whose tractor can pull a heavy sled the farthest.

Driver

Like all other motor sports, the driver must wear a crash helmet and dress from head to toe in flameproof clothing.

Little and large

The huge rear wheels give the tractor as much grip as possible. The front wheels are tiny in comparison. They are only used to steer the tractor. Sometimes they can be lifted clear off the ground.

Huge engines

The engines used in tractor pulling competitions need to be big. Some of the biggest produce a massive 7,000 horsepower—that's more than 11 times the power produced by a Formula One racing car!

Movable weight

During the pull, the weight moves along the sled, toward the tractor. This has the effect of increasing the weight on the drag plate, making it harder for the tractor to pull the sled along.

Control cab

At the rear of the sled sits a referee. He or she sets the speed at which the weight moves forward, making it harder or easier for the tractor to pull the sled. There is also a switch that can turn off the tractor's power in case of an emergency.

Drag plate

At the front of the sled is the drag plate. As the tractor pulls the sled along, this plate is pushed into the ground until it creates so much friction that the tractor is forced to stop.

⚙ LARGE WHEELS

This specially built tractor (right) is fitted with a massive engine and enormous rear wheels to help it drag the large red sled behind it.

ALL SHAPES AND SIZES

Different farms grow different kinds of crops. This means that each farm has different machines to suit their specific needs. For example, a cotton farm needs a cotton picker, but does not need a combine harvester. Just like every farm is different, so too are their machines. Some need to sit up high to fit over the tops of tall plants, while others need to be lower to the ground so that they can dig holes in the soil.

LONG ARM

Sometimes farmers need to pile objects high. To do this, they can use a telescopic handler, which has a long, extendable arm (right).

TRACKED TRACTOR

This tractor (above) is fitted with caterpillar tracks. These tracks reduce the pressure on the ground and therefore reduce the damage the tractor may cause to soil.

DIGGING DRAINS

The massive claw on the front of this bulldozer (above) is sunk into the ground and dragged backward to dig drainage channels. These drainage channels allow water to drain away from a field so the field won't get waterlogged, which damages crops.

TRACTOR ON STILTS

This tractor (below) is raised on specially built axles and suspension. This enables it to raise both itself and spraying equipment above the crop so the chemicals can be sprayed properly.

Bale
A bundle of hay or straw. Rectangular bales can weigh up to 2,200 pounds (1,000 kilograms)!

Caterpillar tracks
These are wide belts that are fixed to a vehicle instead of wheels. They spread the weight of the vehicle over a large area and stop it from damaging the soil too much.

Chaff
Seeds are covered by this protective casing that must be removed before they can be eaten by people.

Cotton boll
Cotton grows in this protective casing that shields the plant's seeds.

Cultivator
This machine is used to further loosen the soil before planting, or to kill weeds after plants have already started to grow.

Double wheels
Large farm machines may have sets of two wheels to spread out the vehicle's weight and prevent it from crushing the soil or plants underneath.

Drag plate
In tractor pulling, this metal plate acts as a brake that causes the tractor to come to a stop when it can no longer pull the weight.

Fodder
Green crops, such as grass or unripe corn, which have been stored for a time in a silo, pit, or open yard. After it has fermented, fodder is used to feed farm animals.

Four-wheel drive
This is when all four wheels on a vehicle are powered by the engine. Four-wheel drive vehicles can pull a heavier load over rougher ground than two-wheel drive vehicles.

Harvester
A machine that collects ripe crops.

Hay baler
Machine that gathers loose hay from the ground and rolls it into a bale that it drops out of a hatch in the back.

Hydraulic machinery
They use liquid to transmit power from the engine to the rest of the machine by increasing or decreasing pressure.

Plow
This machine is used to loosen the soil so that crops are able to grow.

Seed drill
This specialized machine drops seeds into small channels in the soil that it creates with the attached prongs.

Silage
Fodder stored in a high-moisture environment and fed to cud-chewing animals, like cattle and sheep.

Soil
A special type of dirt that is able to support plant life.

Suspension
A system of springs and other devices that makes the ride of a vehicle smoother.

Swath
The row that crops grow in, allowing the machines to pass by without causing damage.

Threshing drum
A barred barrel found inside a combine harvester. As this barrel spins, the bars separate a crop into the grain and the unwanted straw.

Tractor
The most general farm machine that is made to attach to many different tools, allowing it to perform many different functions on the farm.

Trailer
Sometimes a tractor will pull a flat bed trailer behind it to carry crops and other materials.

INDEX

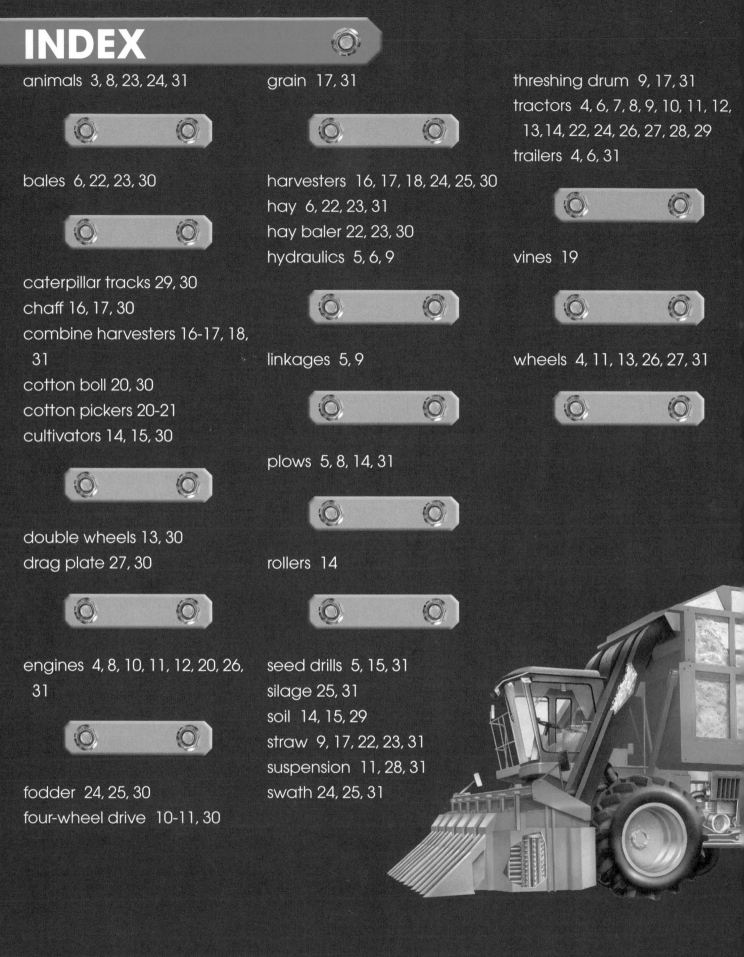

PHOTO CREDITS
Abbreviations: t-top, m-middle, b-bottom, r-right, l-left, c-center.
Pages 4, 6c, 18t, 23, & 29b — Massey Ferguson Tractors. 7t, 13b, & 14t — Renault Agriculture. 19t, & 28b — Charles de Vere. 8, 9t, 13t — Mike Williams/Media Mechanics. 11, 15b, & 25b — JCB Landpower Ltd. 12-13, 14b, 15t, 24b, 25t, & 29 — Peter Hill/Media Mechanics. 17b & 28t — Claas UK. 19b — Spectrum Colour Library. 21 — John Deere. 24t — USDA. 27 — Frank Spooner Pictures.